May Your Birthday Be Filled with the Promise of Good Things to Come

Ellyn Sanna

BARBOUR
PUBLISHING, INC.

*I'm thinking of you
on your special day. . .
and I'm wishing you the best
of everything the future holds.*

Contents

1

Enjoy Your
Special Day!

Most of us can remember a time when a birthday—
especially if it was one's own—
brightened the world as if a second sun had risen.

ROBERT LYND

I'm remembering you on your birthday—

and wishing you a sun-filled day.

It is lovely when I forget all birthdays,
including my own,
to find that somebody remembers me.

ELLEN GLASGOW

Life is so full of meaning and purpose,
so full of beauty,
beneath its covering that you will find
that earth but cloaks your heaven.

FRA GIOVANNI

*May you celebrate today
the many blessings God has given you.*

Let us acknowledge all good,
all delight that the world holds, and be content.

GEORGE MACDONALD

One of the secrets of a happy life
is continuous small treats.

IRIS MURDOCH

On your birthday—and all year round—I pray that your life will be chock-full of special moments. Take time to enjoy life. Don't be so busy you forget to notice a sunset or a child's smile. And be good to yourself. Allow yourself the luxury of small pleasures; things as simple as a walk outdoors, a quiet talk with a friend, or a hot drink in your hand can add so much to life.

I wish you all the happiness the world can hold.

There is something in every season, in every day,
to celebrate with thanksgiving.

GLORIA GAITHER

*May you celebrate all
the possibilities of your day!*

Every day we live is a priceless gift of God,
loaded with possibilities to learn something new,
to gain fresh insights.

DALE EVANS ROGERS

2

Celebrate Yourself!

You may think it seems selfish to celebrate yourself. After all, we've all been taught to be modest, to strive for humility. But the truth is, you are a unique creation of God. In all the world, there's no one else like you; you have the power to demonstrate God's love to the world in a way no other person could ever do.

So what better day to thank God for what He made than today, your birthday? Praise God for all the gifts He gave the world when He created you.

Our God gives you everything you need,
makes you everything you're to be.

2 THESSALONIANS 1:2 THE MESSAGE

What lies behind us and

what lies before us

are tiny matters compared to

what lies within us.

RALPH WALDO EMERSON

One of the greatest steps in discovering who we are is
discovering who God is. . . .
Who we are in Christ is everything.

SHEILA WALSH

Since you are like no other being
ever created since the beginning of time,
you are incomparable.

BRENDA UELAND

*You are God's created beauty and
the focus of His affection and delight.*

JANET L. WEAVER

Our selves may be imperfect, incapable,
and weak, but our souls. . .
are the image of the living God.

MARY HOLLINGSWORTH

Grace means God accepts me just as I am.
He does not require or insist that I measure up to
someone else's standard of performance.
He loves me completely, thoroughly, and perfectly.
There's nothing I can do to add or detract from that love.

MARY GRAHAM

You are precious to God, and today He celebrates your life. Why not join the celebration? Rest in the assurance that God is doing great things in your life. Know that you are loved and treasured by the Creator of the universe.

I'm so glad God made you!

3

Take Pleasure
in Your Age!

Remember when you turned ten? Didn't it seem like the perfect age to be, its impressive two-digits hovering nicely on the edge of childhood? But as we get older, our culture tells us we should begin to be ashamed of the years we have accumulated.

Don't you believe it. God has new things to show you at every age; He has delights and insights, wonders and fulfillment planned for each year of your life. You can grow and learn just as much this year as you did the year you turned ten.

So take pleasure in the age you are right now. It's the perfect age for you to be.

Indeed, now that I come to think of it,
I never really feel grown-up at all.
Perhaps this is because childhood,
catching our imagination when it is fresh and tender,
never lets go of us.

J. B. PRIESTLEY

Childhood is the world of miracle and wonder:
as if creation rose, bathed in light, out of darkness,
utterly new and fresh and astonishing.
The end of childhood is when things cease to astonish us.
When the world seems familiar,
when one has got used to existence,
one has become an adult.

EUGÉNE IONESCO

Time always seems long to the child. . .
when he surrenders his whole soul to
each moment of a happy day.

DAG HAMMARSKJOLD

Oh, the wild joys of living!

the leaping from rock to rock. . .

ROBERT BROWNING

The story of living goes on perpetually.
The days and the years inevitably turn the pages
and open new chapters.

LILIAN WHITING

Our Lord speaks simply: . . .
"Trust Me to pour My love through thee,
as minute succeeds minute."

AMY CARMICHAEL

Don't rob yourself of the joy of
this season by wishing you were
in a future or past one.

CHERYL BIEHL

Consider the lilies how they grow.

LUKE 12:27 KJV

Keep the sky clear. Open wide every avenue of your being to receive the blessed influences your Divine Husbandman may bring to bear upon you. Bask in the sunshine of His love. Drink of the waters of His goodness. Keep your face upturned to Him as the flowers do to the sun. Look, and your soul shall live and grow.

HANNAH WHITALL SMITH

4

Treasure the Years That Have Passed!

Your birthday is a good day to look back at the years that have passed and reflect on all that God has done in your life.

Notice the patterns He created over the years.

Celebrate the memories of love that fill your life.

Rejoice in the years' achievements.

May your memories be birthday gifts of joy.

When we recall the past,
we usually find that it is the simplest things—
not the great occasions—
that in retrospect give off the greatest glow of happiness.

BOB HOPE

Memories are perhaps the best gifts of all.

GLORIA GAITHER

We do not remember days,
we remember moments.
Make moments worth remembering.

CASARE PAVASE

*It is well to drop the old
that one may seize the new.*

LILIAN WHITING

Treasure your memories today—but don't linger in the past, mourning for the "good old days." God's presence was with you each moment of those days, and I know He filled your life with blessings—but He is also with you today.

And He has a storehouse of blessing He still waits to give you in the future.

Christ Jesus has bags of mercy
that have never even been opened.
That is why the Bible says He has goodness laid up. . . .
Who knows what will happen if
He opens just one more of these bags.

JOHN BUNYAN

5

Wishing You a Future Piled High with Gifts!

"For I know the plans I have for you," declares the LORD,
"plans to prosper you and not to harm you,
plans to give you hope and a future."

JEREMIAH 29:11 NIV

Face the future with joy and anticipation.
God has great plans for you!

I don't know what the future holds,
but I know who holds the future.

E. STANLEY JONES

Always begin anew with the day,
just as nature does;
it is one of the sensible things that nature does.

GEORGE E. WOODBERRY

Fill up the crevices of time

with the things that matter most.

AMY CARMICHAEL

If we celebrate the years behind us
they become stepping-stones of strength and joy
for the years ahead.

ANONYMOUS

I love to think that God appoints
My portion day by day;
Events of life are in His hand,
And I would only say,
Appoint them in Thine own good time,
And in Thine own best way.

A. L. WARING

The LORD will guide you always;
he will satisfy your needs. . . .
You will be like a well-watered garden,
like a spring whose waters never fail.

ISAIAH 58:11 NIV

God will never, never, never let us down
if we have faith and put our trust in Him.
He will always look after us.

MOTHER TERESA

Trust in the LORD with all your heart and lean not on your
own understanding;
in all your ways acknowledge him,
and he will make your paths straight.

PROVERBS 3:5–6 NIV

There are better things ahead than any we leave behind.

C. S. LEWIS

Surely goodness and love will follow me
all the days of my life,
and I will dwell in the house
of the LORD forever.

PSALM 23:6 NIV

No eye has seen, nor ear heard,
nor the human heart conceived,
what God has prepared for those who love him.

1 CORINTHIANS 2:9 NRSV

Think of your birthday as a promise from God. Imagine Him speaking the words of Psalm 139 (paraphrased) directly to your heart:

"Look, My child, see what I have created? Before you were ever born, I knew you. I knit you together in your mother's womb, making you complex and perfect; My workmanship was marvelous! Before your birth, I recorded every day of your life in My book; I laid out the moments and filled them full of blessings. Those past moments were my gift to you—but I have more gifts I long to give you. For I both precede and follow you; I place My hand of blessing on your head as I lead you along the path of everlasting life. My thoughts of you are precious to Me. You will never be separated from My spirit."

I wish you sunshine on your path and storms to season your journey. I wish you peace—in the world in which you live and in the smallest corner of the heart where truth is kept. I wish you faith—to help define your living and your life. More I cannot wish you—except perhaps love—to make all the rest worthwhile.

ROBERT A. WARD

It is God to whom and with whom we travel, and while He is the End of our journey, He is also at every stopping place.

ELISABETH ELLIOT

Time is a precious gift of God;
so precious that it's only given to us moment by moment.

AMELIA BARR

*Time with your heavenly Father
is never wasted.*

EMILIE BARNES

The LORD is faithful to all his promises
and loving toward all he has made.

PSALM 145:13 NIV

Trust in the LORD with all your heart;
do not depend on your own understanding.
Seek his will in all you do,
and he will direct your paths.

PROVERBS 3:5–6 NLT

Take delight in the LORD,

and he will give you your heart's desires.

PSALM 37:4 NLT

He is first, and He is last!
And we are gathered up in between,
as in great arms of eternal lovingkindness.

AMY CARMICHAEL

*"I am Alpha and Omega,
the first and the last."*

REVELATION 1:11 KJV

The LORD will go before you,
the God of Israel will be your rear guard.

ISAIAH 52:12 NIV

We see hardly one inch
of the narrow lane of time.
To our God,
eternity lies open as a meadow.

AMY CARMICHAEL

I will answer them before they even call to me.
While they are still talking about their needs,
I will go ahead and answer their prayers!

ISAIAH 65:24 NLT

Occasionally I must remind myself
that all gifts are given to me,
God's beloved child, with incomparable love and joy. . . .
Everything good and loving in life has its source in God,
including all gifts.

MARILYN MEBERG

*As you enjoy your gifts today, remember—
the greatest gift of all is the gift of love!*

Lord, may no gift of Yours ever take Your place in my heart.
Help me to hold them lightly in an open palm.

ELISABETH ELLIOT

I wish you all the joy that you can wish.

WILLIAM SHAKESPEARE

Please know my heart is filled with thoughts of you today. I'm praying that you will. . .
   have a wonderful day!
      thank God for all He's done in your life!
         enjoy your memories of the past!
            and take delight in the future's promise!

Happy birthday!